PART ONE

CHAPTER ONE

BRAHMIN

CONTENTS

PART ONE

1/ BRAHMIN
7

2/ TATTA THE URCHIN
59

3/ GENERAL BUDAI
105

4/ THE ANNOUNCEMENT
147

5/ CHAPRA
161

6/ THE KING'S CUP
211

7/ THE BIRTH
249

8/ THE CONTEST
275

9/ ALL FOR A CURE
305

10/ THE PROPHECY
335

11/ THE JUDGMENT
357

12/ THE WALL OF DEATH
385

VERTICAL

1: *Kapilavastu*

OSAMU TEZUKA

BUDDHA

THE JOURNEY

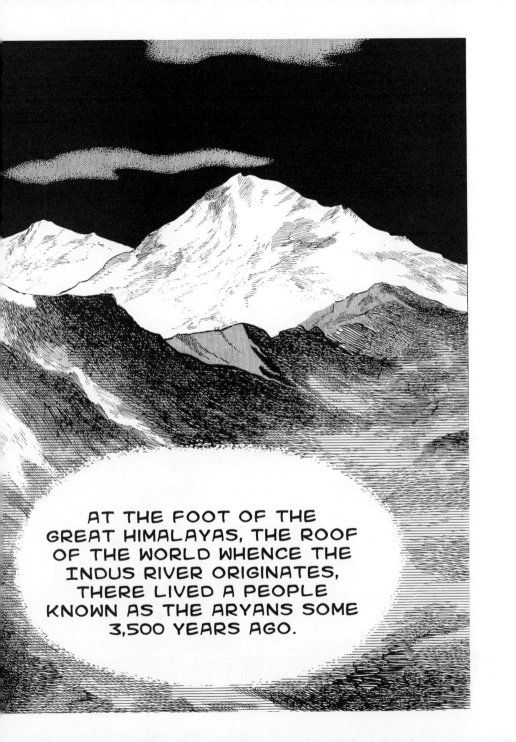

AT THE FOOT OF THE GREAT HIMALAYAS, THE ROOF OF THE WORLD WHENCE THE INDUS RIVER ORIGINATES, THERE LIVED A PEOPLE KNOWN AS THE ARYANS SOME 3,500 YEARS AGO.

BATTLING DRIVING RAIN, HARSH WINDS,

AND DEVASTATING DROUGHTS, THEY PUSHED SOUTH, SPREADING THEIR CULTURE INTO WHAT WOULD LATER BECOME INDIA.

AMONG THE ARYAN
CONQUERORS,
THE PUREST
OF BLOOD BECAME
THE LEADERS OF
SOCIETY. THEY CALLED
THEMSELVES BRAHMIN.

BRAHMIN! THE VERY NAME WAS AN EMBLEM
OF INVINCIBLE POWER IN INDIAN SOCIETY
FOR CENTURIES.

UNDERNEATH THEM THE BRAHMIN
CREATED CLASSES LIKE
"WARRIOR," "COMMONER," AND "SLAVE,"
INTRODUCING DISCRIMINATION AMONG
FELLOW HUMANS.

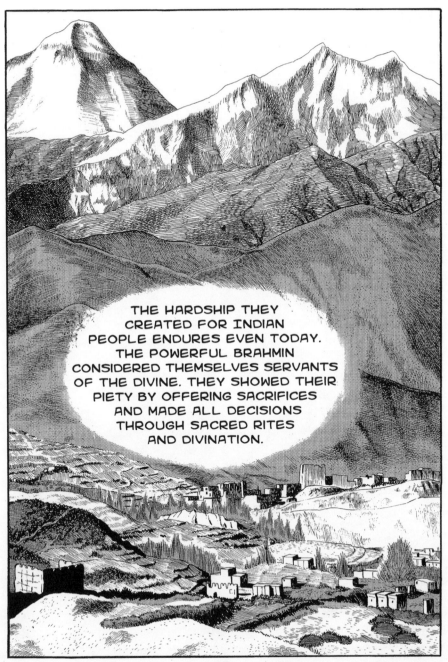

THE HARDSHIP THEY CREATED FOR INDIAN PEOPLE ENDURES EVEN TODAY. THE POWERFUL BRAHMIN CONSIDERED THEMSELVES SERVANTS OF THE DIVINE. THEY SHOWED THEIR PIETY BY OFFERING SACRIFICES AND MADE ALL DECISIONS THROUGH SACRED RITES AND DIVINATION.

THEY BECAME VAIN AND DECADENT, AND THEIR RELIGIOUS CELEBRATIONS DEGENERATED TO MERE FORM.

PEOPLE GREW DISSATISFIED WITH BRAHMIN SHAMMING AND BEGAN SEEKING ALTERNATE PATHS TO HAPPINESS AND PEACE OF MIND.

THEY WAITED AND WAITED FOR A NEW TEACHER.

16

BUT MASTER ASITA, IT CAN'T BE TRUE! A RABBIT IMMOLATING HIMSELF SO THAT HE CAN BE EATEN BY A HUMAN?!

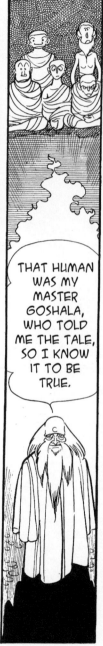

THAT HUMAN WAS MY MASTER GOSHALA, WHO TOLD ME THE TALE, SO I KNOW IT TO BE TRUE.

HE HIMSELF WAS SO SHAKEN BY THE UNBELIEVABLE EVENT THAT...

27

THIS RIDDLE OF THE SELF-SACRIFICING RABBIT

NOT EVEN MASTER ASITA KNOWS THE ANSWER?

 THERE ARE BUT FEW WHO CAN SOLVE THE RIDDLE.

 HE WHO CAN HAS THE POWER TO BECOME A GOD, OR RULER OF THE WORLD.

MUMBLE MUMBLE PSST

 SO WHERE IS HE?

 NO, ONE DAY HE WILL SURELY APPEAR.

 I KNOW NOT.

SO YOU WERE JUST KIDDING?

STRAIGHT SOUTH, HUH?

IF MASTER ASITA PREDICTED TRULY, I MAY SEE WITH MY OWN EYES A FUTURE GOD...

A RARE CHANCE INDEED...

HUFF HUFF

EAT ME IF YOU MUST... I AM PREPARED.

PHEW...

STRANGE. THAT TIGER ATTACKED, BUT RETREATED WITHOUT EATING ME.

AND THOSE EYES.

MAY I HAVE A BOWL OF WATER?

HERE YOU ARE.

32

WHERE YA FROM, YOUNG BRAHMIN?

UP NORTH IN THE MOUNTAINS. SAY, DO YOU KNOW OF ANYONE AROUND WITH STRANGE POWERS?

YOU MEAN LIKE ESP?

YES, I SUPPOSE.

THERE'S A MONK WHO IS UNDERTAKING HARDSHIPS UNDER THAT BANYAN TREE.

HE CAN USE MAGIC.

IT CAN'T HURT TO LOOK INTO THIS.

HEY, WAIT UP! THAT'S SOME NASTY GASH YOU'VE GOT...

I ENCOUN-TERED A TIGER ON MY WAY HERE.

TIGER?!

YES, A TIGER. WHAT'S WRONG?

......
......

33

IT WAS A STRANGE TIGER. HE ATTACKED, BUT DIDN'T EVEN TRY TO BITE ME...

HE TURNED AROUND AND LET ME BE.

... ... THAT TIGER IS...

NOTHING, FORGET IT!

O MASSES WHO BELIEVE IN SPIRITS, BEHOLD MY POWER AND CLEANSE YOURSELVES OF IMPURITY!

PLINK

PLINK

Whoosh

OOH... AH...

... ...

34

35

I—I DIDN'T REALIZE...

YOU WERE A FOLLOWER OF THE FAMOUS ASITA.

FORGIVE ME... IF LIFE WEREN'T SO CRUEL, I WOULDN'T BE DOING THIS.

YOU'RE STILL YOUNG AND MAY NOT UNDER- STAND,

BUT I'VE GOT NO OTHER CHOICE, HE HE HE ...

HOW DIS- APPOINTING. I'VE COME HERE FROM UP NORTH...

TO FIND A MYSTERIOUS MAN WITH SPECIAL POWERS.

THERE'S NO BRAHMIN LIKE THAT...

WHAT DOES THAT MEAN?

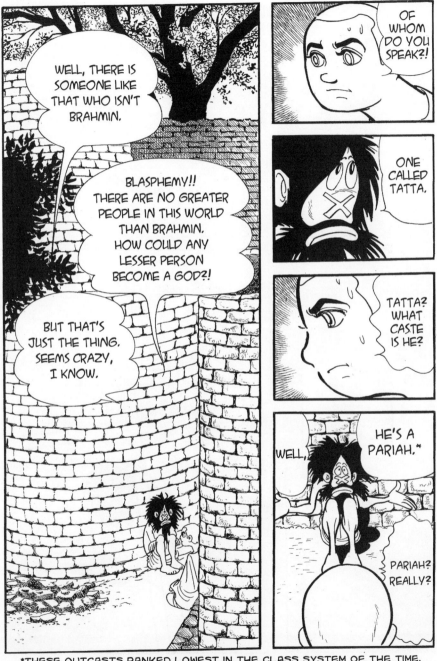

*THESE OUTCASTS RANKED LOWEST IN THE CLASS SYSTEM OF THE TIME, LOWER EVEN THAN SHUDRA, THE SLAVE CASTE. CONSIDERED SUBHUMAN, PARIAHS SUFFERED TERRIBLE DISCRIMINATION.

OK, OUT OF RESPECT FOR YOUR MOTHER, I'LL GRANT YOU 3 DAYS TO GET THE GOODS BACK.

TH-THANK YOU!

THANK GOODNESS.

BUT IF I DON'T HAVE THEM BACK IN 3 DAYS, I'M SELLING YOUR MOTHER OFF! GOT IT?

WHAT'S GOOD? HE'S GOING TO SELL YOU OFF!

DON'T WORRY ABOUT ME, HONEY. COME NOW.

BE CAREFUL. HERE'S 3 DAYS' WORTH OF FOOD.

MOTHER... I-I'M COMING BACK WITH THE GOODS!

ALREADY
DAY 3 ...

AND
NOT
EVEN
A LEAD.

WHAT'S SO FUNNY?!
I'VE BEEN LOOKING
FOR 3 DAYS...

IF I DON'T
BRING THE STUFF
BACK MY MOTHER'S
GONNA BE SOLD!!

GUFFAW HA HA HA HEE HEE HEE

47

OWWW

AAAAGH!

GET 'IM!!

FREEZE!

......

THAT WAS JUST A WARM-UP. DON'T YOU DARE!!

NEVER SEEN THAT BEFORE. WHERE'D YA LEARN TO THROW LIKE THAT?

I TAUGHT MYSELF TRYING TO CATCH TURTLEDOVES.

THIS TIME I'LL AIM FOR YER NOSES!

50

THAT'LL DO. NO POINT IN KILLIN' HIM.

SHALL WE TOSS HIM OUT?

TAKE HIM TO MY PLACE.

HUH?

WHY NOT HANG 'IM UP IN THE STREET?

DO WHAT I SAY!!

THIS MUST BE TATTA'S HOME.

WOW... IT'S WORSE THAN A PIG STY...

53

ALL DONE, MAMA.

WRAP THIS AROUND YOU!

IT'S A BIT LOUD...

HEY! THAT'S MY CLOTH!

OW-OW-OUCH

WHAT DID YOU DO WITH IT?!

THIEF! SCUM! GIVE IT BACK!!

OH, IT'S PERFECT ON YOU. YOU LOOK LIKE A STAR!

55

SHUT UP, BEAST!!

HERE'S HOW IT IS: THE KING TAKES FROM OFFICIALS, WHO TAKE FROM TOWNSFOLK...

TOWNSFOLK ROB SLAVES, WHO PILFER BEGGARS!

SO WHO DO BEGGARS TAKE FROM?

WHO IS THERE BELOW US?!

WHAT'S THE RACKET ABOUT?

HE SAYS HE WANTS THE PRETTY DRESS I MADE FOR MOM.

HE'S STILL WHINING?

Y-YOU...

THIS IS OUR VILLAGE.

MESS WITH IT...

AND WE'LL COOK YOU AND HAVE YOU FOR DINNER. HE HE HE HE

HE'S CRYING.

HA, NICE TRY!

MY MOTHER'S GOING TO BE SOLD TONIGHT! I MIGHT NEVER SEE HER AGAIN...

IF I DON'T RETURN THE GOODS TONIGHT... OUR MASTER WILL SELL HER OFF!!

...

YOU DON'T KNOW WHAT IT'S LIKE TO BE A SLAVE!!

YOU MAY BE OF LOW BIRTH AND MISTREATED, TOO,

BUT AT LEAST YOU CAN BE WITH YOUR MOTHER.

IMAGINE YOUR MOTHER BEING SOLD OFF LIKE A COW OR PIG...

OH NO...

SHOULD WE GO HELP YOUR MOM?

DID YOU SAY "HELP"?

YOU WON'T GIVE BACK WHAT YOU STOLE, BUT YOU'LL HELP HER?!

AND IN RETURN, YOU TWO DON'T EVER HAVE TO GO BACK TO YOUR MASTER.

IT'LL BE A MIRACLE IF WE CAN SAVE HER...

HEH HEH

CHAPTER TWO

TATTA THE URCHIN

THEY'RE HEADED FOR THE SLAVE MARKET IN THE NEXT TOWN...

RESCUE HER QUICK!

HEH HEH HEH, NOT YET...

YOU SEE THE FIELD UP AHEAD?

CHAPRA, NO MATTER WHAT HAPPENS, STAY HERE AND KEEP STILL.

WH- WHAT'S GONNA HAPPEN?

YOU AREN'T GONNA...

KILL THE MERCHANT? MAYBE!

TATTA!

WHOOSH

RUSTLE RUSTLE RUSTLE

TATTA, YOU CAN TURN YOURSELF INTO A TIGER?!

ALL I DID WAS POSSESS ONE.

POSSESS A TIGER?

NO WAY!

YOU SHOULD TAKE CARE OF YOUR MOTHER NOW.

I'LL EXPLAIN LATER.

MOTHER!!

OH... CHA- CHAPRA!

THANK GOODNESS, MOTHER... YOU'RE SAFE NOW.

HONEY... WHAT... I CAN'T SEEM TO...

A TIGER...

71

WHEN I'M SAD, I CRY WITH THEM. WHEN I'M IN PAIN, WE MOAN TOGETHER...

I WISH I'D BEEN BORN AS ONE OF THEM.

SOME YEARS BACK...

I WAS BEATEN TO A PULP AND LEFT FOR DEAD IN THIS FIELD BY SOME BASTARDS.

I NEEDED WATER BAD.

A TIGER CAME AND STARED AT ME.

I STARED BACK, AND WISHED I COULD BECOME THE TIGER SO I COULD GET SOME WATER...

I HAD A WEIRD FEELING...

AND SUDDENLY I WAS THERE,

INSIDE THE TIGER.

I LOOKED AT MYSELF, A TIGER.

AND MY HUMAN BODY LAY THERE LIKE A RAG DOLL.

I RAN! FAST! I WAS STRONG!

THEN I CARRIED MY HUMAN BODY OVER TO THE WATER.

CAN YOU ONLY POSSESS TIGERS? HOW ABOUT OTHER ANIMALS?

BIRDS, RABBITS, SNAKES, ANY ANIMAL THAT HAS A SOUL. I CAN'T DO IT WITH BUGS, THOUGH. THEIR MINDS DON'T WORK THE SAME.

BIRDS ARE COOL, MAN. NOTHIN' LIKE SPREADING YOUR WINGS AND SOARING.

THAT'S SO COOL!! CAN YOU TEACH ME?

THIS AIN'T NO TRICK, DUDE. YOU EITHER GOT IT OR YOU DON'T.

SO HOW DO YOU GET IT?

HMM, DUNNO.

BUT...

I BET YOU HAVE TO HIT ROCK BOTTOM AND START WONDERING IF YOU AREN'T JUST A BEAST AFTER ALL.

76

HEY SON, HOW FAR TO THE CITY OF KAPILAVASTU?

THREE TOWNS OVER.

REPORT THAT TO THE MAIN FORCE. THEY MAY ADVANCE!

I'LL SEE TO THESE THREE.

TO THE WALL.

WHAT ARE YOU...

STAND AGAINST THE WALL!!

YOU'RE GOING TO KILL US?!!

WHY NOT?

EASIER THAN KILLING THREE WORMS.

I CAN'T HAVE YOU GO ALERT THE CITY.

WORMS?

HIYAH!!

BAM!

ARGH!

AH

YOU OK, TATTA?

IT'S NOTHIN'...

COMPARED TO DYING.

SO BRAVE FOR A CHILD.

CHILD? I'M 7 ALREADY!

WHICH WAY'D THEY GO?

DOESN'T MATTER TO ME.

GULP

TOWARD OUR TOWN!! NO!!

MOM!

SIS!

THE PARIAH VILLAGE IS ON THE OUTSKIRTS OF TOWN!!

LOOK AT THAT SMOKE...

THEY'VE SET THE TOWN ON FIRE! YO, HUMANS AREN'T BARBECUE MEAT!

HEY!! EVERYONE OK?

TATTA, IT'S HORRIBLE...

THEY USED FLAMING ARROWS. M—MOST EVERYBODY'S DEAD.

OUR HOUSE!

TATTA, YOU'LL DIE IN THERE TOO!

COME OUT!

OHH...

AAAH...

WEEP WEEP WEEP

KISS
KISS

TATTA, I'M SORRY ...

LEAVE ME ALONE!!

HONEY, THERE'S JUST ONE PLACE TO HIDE: BEHIND THE MASTER'S HOUSE IN THE WINE CELLAR. IT'S SAFE FROM THE FIRE AND THE SOLDIERS.

LET'S GO!

89

HERE YOU GO.

I'M IMPRESSED, MOM.

I HAD TO CARRY LIQUOR FOR PARTIES FROM HERE.

NO ONE'LL FIND US NOW...

NO MATTER WHAT HAPPENS, WE WON'T BE SEPARATED AGAIN.

HONEY, NOT IN FRONT OF THE OTHERS.

92

WELCOME! YOU'VE HAD SOME BAD LUCK.

BUT NOT TO WORRY. OUR ARMY WON'T HARM BRAHMIN.

I AM NARADATTA, A DISCIPLE OF MASTER ASITA.

MASTER ASITA? AH YES, I'VE HEARD OF HIM.

TRANSFORMS REGULAR TAP WATER INTO COLA, RIGHT?

OH DEAR, NOT THIS AGAIN.

I AM SEARCHING FOR SOMEONE AT HIS ORDERS.

I AM GENERAL BUDAI OF KOSALA, STATE YOUR QUERY.

GENERAL, THE MASTER SAYS THAT...

A GREAT MAN LIVES IN THIS VICINITY.

IT IS HIS BIRTHRIGHT TO BECOME A GOD,

OR PERHAPS HE IS TO BECOME KING OF THE WORLD.

KING OF THE WORLD?

WORLD?

HA HA HA HA, I LIKE THAT!

Ha Ha

Ho Ho

94

THE GREATEST RULER IN THE WORLD IS KOSALA'S KING. YOU SAY THERE'S ONE GREATER?

HA!

THAT'S A BAD JOKE, BRAHMIN!

IMPOSSIBLE!

I'M A SOLDIER LOYAL TO MY KING AND WE ARE ON THE WARPATH!

PULLING BACK WOULD MEAN...

IN ANY CASE, THIS PERSON WILL APPEAR NEAR HERE.

BY ATTACKING THIS LAND, YOU DRAW YOUR SWORD AGAINST HIM.

YOU MUST PULL BACK, GENERAL!

RETREAT!

DEFEAT? RETREAT?

TAKE THEM ALL.

A—ALL OF THEM?

YEP.

THE SOLDIERS NEED A BREAK!

THIS LOOKS LIKE THE BEST.

FOR OUR SIRE.

WON'T YOU JOIN ME IN A DRINK, BRAHMIN? HEH HEH HEH

SO STIFF FOR A YOUNG MAN. WHY NOT THINK OF IT AS A HEAVENLY GIFT AND DRINK UP?

SUCH A GRUMPY MONK.

WHISH

ARGH!

WH— WHAT THE...?

UGH!

YOU GOT SOME NERVE KILLING MY MOTHER AND SISTER, MURDERER!

99

MONK, LEMME BE.

HEH...I'M JUST A PARIAH, NOT EVEN HUMAN.

I DON'T UNDERSTAND IT MYSELF, BUT YOU MUST NOT DIE!

YOU ARE OUT OF YOUR MIND.

SO BE IT, BRAHMIN, DIE WITH HIM.

MR. MONK, ARE THERE CASTES EVEN AFTER WE DIE?

YOU'RE HIGH CASTE.

FUNNY WE SHOULD DIE THE SAME DEATH, ALL TIED UP.

CHAPRA, WHEREVER YOU ARE! I GO FIRST!

CHAPTER THREE

GENERAL BUDAI

MOTHER, WE'VE GOT TO HELP TATTA.

I CAN'T JUST WATCH HIM DIE.

TO-NIGHT'S A FULL MOON.

THE DAY AFTER THE FULL MOON IN AUGUST, THE LOCUSTS BEGIN MOVING.

IF ONLY THEY SWOOP DOWN AT DAWN...

YOU'RE GOING TO COUNT ON THAT?

I BELIEVE IN LUCK!

IT'S SUCH A LONG SHOT.

THE FIRST TEN! AIM!

SHOOT!

THWACK

THWACK

ARGH

ECH

TATTA!!

BRO!

RUN QUICK!

THIS MONK HERE TOO.

RUN!

THERE EXISTS A TYPE OF
LOCUST THAT, WHEN
FOOD SOURCES RUN DRY,
TRAVEL TOGETHER IN A
SWARM TO SEEK MORE
HOSPITABLE TURF.
ON A CERTAIN SIGNAL,
THE SWARM RISES UP,
CREATING A CLOUD-
LIKE MASS SO BIG IT
NEARLY OBLITERATES
THE SUN. THEY NUMBER
SO MANY THAT THE
MIGRATION TAKES
SEVERAL DAYS. WHEN
THEY FINALLY DESCEND
ON PLANT LIFE FAR AWAY,
IT IS AS IF A STORM
HAS COME TO LIFE.
(FROM J.H. FABRE'S
"THE STORY OF SCIENCE.")

TREES

GRAIN

CROPS

ANY AND ALL PLANTS

ARE CONSUMED BY THE SWARM.

115

FOR HUMANS, LIVESTOCK, AND ALL THE ANIMALS OF THE HILLS AND FIELDS, THE SWARM MEANS DEATH. LOCUSTS HAVE CAUSED RUINOUS FAMINE SEVERAL TIMES IN ALGERIA.

EVEN TODAY, IN THE ERA OF SCIENCE,

WE HAVE NO WAY OF COUNTERING THIS NATURAL THREAT.

FOR PEOPLE OF YORE,

THERE WAS NOTHING TO DO IN THE FACE OF CALAMITY AND PESTILENCE BUT TO PRAY AND WEEP.

PRAY? TO WHOM? PRIESTS TOLD YOU TO WHOM.

PFFT PFFT PFFT PFFT PFFT PFFT

MONKS AND PRIESTS EXPLAINED THAT NATURE'S MYSTERIES AND TERRIFYING POWER WERE THE WORK OF GODS. THEY TAUGHT PEOPLE TO CELEBRATE, SERVE AND PRAY TO THESE GODS.

BUT DID THAT HELP THEM ESCAPE MISFORTUNE?

118

I'VE TAKEN A LOOK AROUND ...

THE FIELDS ARE BARE! THEY WERE WORSE THAN FIRE!

NOT A BLADE OF GRASS, NOR A SINGLE POPPY SEED! LOTS OF DEAD LOCUSTS, THOUGH.

ANY WATER?

SPLASH
PLOP

THE RIVER'S A LOCUST GRAVEYARD! TOTALLY POISONED!

WHAT'S BECOME OF THE SOLDIERS?

WHO CARES ABOUT THEM?!

I'M SURE THEY'RE LOOKING FOR US.

LET'S GO TO KAPILA-VASTU. IF WE MAKE IT THERE...

ENOUGH!

I'VE HAD IT!!

WHY DO WE HAVE TO GO THROUGH THIS HELL!!

DAY AFTER DAY WE SUFFER FOR BEING UNDERCLASS, AND AS IF WAR HASN'T MADE THINGS BAD ENOUGH FOR US, LOCUSTS SPOIL EVEN OUR WATER!!

WHAT'S THE POINT OF LIFE? WHY'D YOU GIVE BIRTH TO ME, MOM? HUH?

WHAT FOR ?!

I-I'M SORRY MOTHER.

MY DEAR BOY.

MOTHER, WHY CAN'T WE BE FREE AT LEAST ?

121

I KNOW.

I'M GOING TO HIDE THAT I'M A SLAVE.

I'LL MOVE UP IN THE WORLD.

BUT YOU CAN'T.

A SLAVE IS A SLAVE. NO MATTER WHERE YOU GO, THAT'LL NEVER CHANGE.

WHY? WHAT IF I DON'T TELL ANYONE?

LOOK AT YOUR FOOT.

THAT BRAND CAN'T BE ERASED. THEY'LL KNOW.

RATS!!

STAMP

STAMP

I'LL CUT OFF MY FOOT THEN!!

MOTHER, JUST WAIT AND SEE. ONE DAY I'M GOING TO DRESS YOU IN GOLD AND GIVE YOU A PALACE WITH A POOL AND MAKE-UP CHAMBER! I SWEAR!!

I PROMISE!!

OH, MY BOY!

HEY, CHAPRA!! WE GOT SOMETHING HERE!

CHECK IT OUT.

IT'S GRAIN! FOOD!

GIVE ME THAT!

WE'LL HAVE EQUAL PORTIONS: ME, MOTHER, YOU AND THE MONK.

NOT SO FAST. THAT'S NOT ALL OF US.

THESE FIELD MICE! THEY LED US TO THE FOOD IN THE FIRST PLACE.

ARE YOU KIDDING?

THESE ANIMALS ARE MY PEEPS.

AS YOU LIKE, LITTLE BRO.

YOU SPLIT IT UP THEN.

WHAT? THERE ARE OTHERS OUTSIDE TOO?

125

FOR YOU, MOMS.

AND YOU, MR. MONK.

WHAT'S WITH THE BLANK STARE?

YOU'VE BEEN AWFULLY QUIET.

YOU ARE WONDERFUL!!

I WAS NOT MIS-TAKEN.

YOU ARE NOT LIKE THE REST OF US.

A PARIAH, AND YET... WHY?

WHAT-EVER.

HEY, TATTA!

YOU THINK THIS HORSE COULD TAKE ME TO THE SOLDIERS?

127

TATTA
...

YO,
TATTA.

AN
EMPTY
SHELL.

THUD

TATTA!!

NEIGH

YOUR SON JUST TOOK OFF ON HORSEBACK.

WHAT?

TATTA! OH DEAR...

WAKE UP!

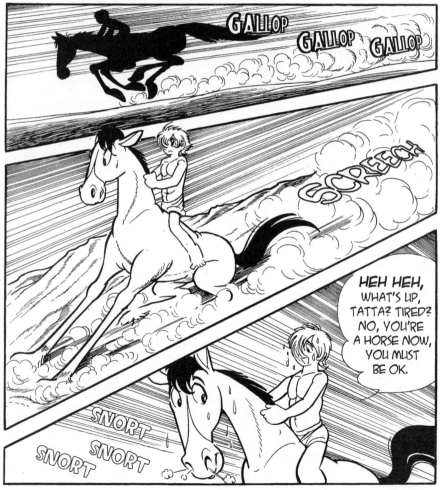

GALLOP GALLOP GALLOP

SCREECH

HEH HEH, WHAT'S UP, TATTA? TIRED? NO, YOU'RE A HORSE NOW, YOU MUST BE OK.

SNORT SNORT SNORT

ALL OUR SUPPLIES AND THE TOWN'S HAVE BEEN DECIMATED BY THE LOCUSTS, SIR.

HMPH, WE COULD NOT HAVE BEEN MORE UNLUCKY. OUR PLAN IS TO ATTACK THE CASTLE OF KAPILAVASTU TOMORROW!

HAVE YOU EVER TRIED LOCUST? THEY'RE PRETTY TASTY.

IDIOT!

I NEED A BATH. IS THERE A RIVER NEARBY?

IT'S SLICK WITH DEAD LOCUSTS. NO GOOD FOR THAT.

131

THERE'S A NATURAL SPRING IN THE VALLEY TO THE NORTHWEST. IT MIGHT BE CLEAN.

READY MY HORSE.

Pok

Pok

Pok

Pok

Pok

WHOA, IT'S COLD. OOOH-AH! FEELS GOOD!

135

137

140

HALT, YOU.

SIRE!!

WHAT DID YOU DO TO HIM?

HE WAS ATTACKED BY CROCODILES WHILE HE WAS BATHING. I SAVED HIM AND AM RETURNING HIM TO YOU.

GET IT?

WOW

WAIT HERE.

ARE YOU THE ONE WHO BROUGHT BACK HIS EXCELLENCY? HE HAS REGAINED CONSCIOUSNESS.

HE WANTS TO SEE YOU

Y-YOU ... ...

SAVED MY LIFE... I THANK YOU

BE MY... S-SON... I'VE GOT NO... CHILDREN...

BE YOUR SON ???

Y-YES WHOEVER YOU MAY BE

I HAVE NO GREATER GIFT TO OFFER... PLEASE ACCEPT

ME, YOUR HEIR, GENERAL?! OF COURSE!

I WILL!

I WILL BE YOUR SON!

CHAPTER FOUR

THE ANNOUNCEMENT

THE ARMY OF KOSALA,
LED BY GENERAL BUDAI,
HAD COME TO STORM
THE LITTLE CASTLE OF
KAPILAVASTU. TWO TRIBES,
THE SHAKYA AND THE KOLIYA,
LIVED IN HARMONY ON
EITHER SHORE OF THE
ROHINI RIVER. KAPILAVASTU
WAS THE CAPITAL
OF THE SHAKYA.

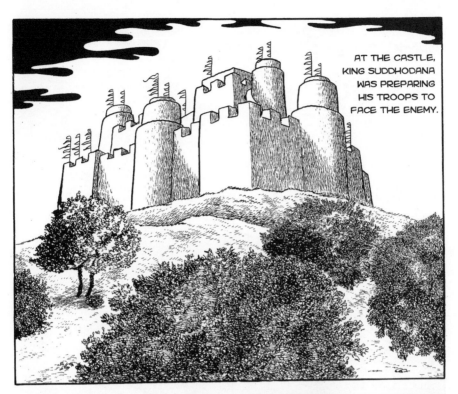

AT THE CASTLE, KING SUDDHODANA WAS PREPARING HIS TROOPS TO FACE THE ENEMY.

LONG LIVE THE KING

150

GLORY BE.
THIS IS DIVINE
PROVIDENCE.

152

A NOBLE WHITE ELEPHANT WITH 6 TUSKS GENTLY ENTERS MY BODY UNDER MY LEFT ARM.

ONCE A MONTH I HAVE THAT SAME DREAM.

AND YOU BECAME PREGNANT THE FIRST TIME YOU HAD IT.

YES...

SOME-THING STRANGE HAS HAPPENED TO ME, TOO.

TWO MONTHS AGO I QUIT HUNTING ALTOGETHER... AS YOU KNOW WELL,

I'D NEVER LET ANY ANIMAL SLIP AWAY. AND THAT DAY TOO I'D HOPED TO COME ACROSS SOME NIMBLE DEER.

AND I DID! I DREW MY BOW, BUT...

THE DEER DIDN'T RUN. INSTEAD IT CAME TOWARD ME, WITH FRIENDSHIP IN ITS EYES.

WHEN I LOOKED AROUND, IT WASN'T JUST THE DEER. SQUIRRELS, RABBITS, BIRDS, THEY WERE ALL SMILING AT ME. THEY DREW NEAR AS IF I WERE A KINDRED SPIRIT.

I TRIED TO DRAW MY BOW ONCE MORE, BUT MY HANDS SHOOK

THE THRILL OF HUNTING LIES IN THE CHASE, MAYA. IT'S NOT POSSIBLE TO KILL ANIMALS THAT DRAW NEAR.

AND SO I LOST MY TASTE FOR HUNTING ...

155

WHAT'S TO ACCOUNT FOR THESE STRANGE EVENTS? THE ELEPHANT DREAM, THE ANIMALS.

AND NOW THE LOCUST SWARM!

MAYA, I CANNOT HELP BUT THINK THAT ALL THESE THINGS MUST BE CONNECTED TO THE CHILD IN YOUR WOMB.

IT SEEMS THAT IT'LL BE NO ORDINARY BABY...

STOP THIS, DEAR.

THIS BABY IS MY BABY.

A HEALTHY CHILD IS ALL I HOPE FOR.

I FEEL THE CHILD WILL GROW UP TO BE A SPECIAL PERSON.

OF COURSE! HE'LL BE YOUR HEIR!

NO, I MEAN...

SOMEONE WHO WILL CHANGE THE WORLD, EVEN.

I FEEL IT IN MY BONES.

MAYA, TAKE CARE OF YOUR-SELF.

IT'S STILL 4 MONTHS AWAY.

RIGHT DURING THE DRY SEASON ...

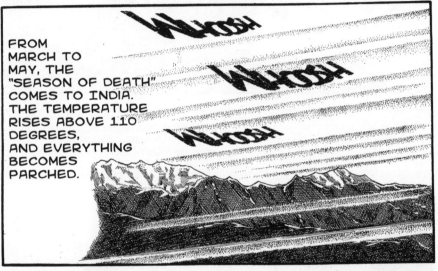

FROM MARCH TO MAY, THE "SEASON OF DEATH" COMES TO INDIA. THE TEMPERATURE RISES ABOVE 110 DEGREES, AND EVERYTHING BECOMES PARCHED.

WHOOSH

WHOOSH

WHOOSH

SANDSTORMS AND TORNADOES SWIRL, GRASS AND TREES WILT, RIVERS RUN DRY, AND THEN COME THE EPIDEMICS, ALL IN THE 110-PLUS DEGREE HEAT.

IN THE MIDST OF THE DROUGHT, STORMS AND PESTILENCE, LARGE NUMBERS OF INDIANS USED TO STARVE TO DEATH. DESPITE SUCH HARDSHIP, THE PEOPLE ALWAYS MANAGED TO BOUNCE BACK.

NO MATTER HOW DEVOUT THE BRAHMIN, NO MATTER HOW BENEVOLENT THE KING, THE PEOPLE COULD NOT ESCAPE THIS FATE.

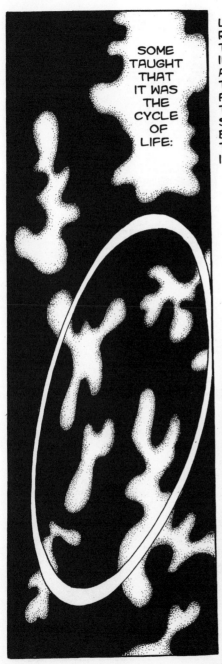

SOME TAUGHT THAT IT WAS THE CYCLE OF LIFE:

LIVING THINGS RECEIVE LIFE, THEN DIE, AND IN DEATH ARE REBORN. THEY ARE FATED NEVER TO ESCAPE SUFFERING BECAUSE THE CYCLE IS ETERNAL.

WHY DO HUMANS SUFFER?
WHY DO THEY LIVE?
WHY SHOULD A WORLD
SUCH AS OURS EXIST?
WHY DID THE UNIVERSE
GIVE BIRTH TO IT?

PEOPLE SOUGHT ANSWERS
TO THESE QUESTIONS.
AND SOON, THE ONE WHO
HELD THE KEY TO THE
RIDDLES WOULD APPEAR.
IN FOUR MONTHS' TIME,
THAT GREAT ONE WAS TO
RECEIVE LIFE UPON EARTH.

CHAPTER FIVE

CHAPRA

AT-TEN-SHUN!
HIS EXCELLENCY
THE GENERAL!

162

ROYAL GUARDS! AS YOU CAN SEE, I HAVE COMPLETELY RECOVERED.

UNFORTUNATELY, I LOST AN ARM AND A LEG TO THE CROCODILES.

BUT!

I'VE GAINED SOMETHING MUCH MORE WONDERFUL THAN A LIMB:

A SON!!

LET ME INTRODUCE MY SON, CHAPRA.

NICE TO MEET YOU...

CAPTAIN! YOU'LL TRAIN CHAPRA.

YESSIR!

STUDY HARD, MY SON.

I WILL.

164

166

THAT WASN'T FAIR!

ALL'S FAIR IN LOVE AND WAR. FIGHT DIRTY IF YOU LIKE, KID... COME ON.

OHHH

WENT EASY ON ME, DID YOU, BRAT? I'LL TEACH YOU NOT TO TALK LIKE THAT!

SQUISH!

UGH...

THAT'S ALL FOR TODAY.

ONE OF YOU, MAKE SURE HE'S BREATHING.

GUFFAW

GUFFAW

HA HA HA

HEY, LAD, SIT HERE.

EAT UP. WHAT'S THE LONG FACE FOR?

I DON'T THINK I'M CUT OUT TO BE A ROYAL GUARD...

CUT OUT?

NOBODY'S CUT OUT AT FIRST.

DON'T WORRY. THEY'RE ALL GOOD GUYS. YOU'LL BE ON PAR WITH THEM ONE DAY.

HOW'D YOU GET TO BE THE GENERAL'S SON ANYWAY?

175

THE GENERAL WAS SWIMMING IN A POND WHEN THREE CROCS ATTACKED HIM.

YES, WITH A BOW.

YOU TELLING ME YOU GOT ALL THREE?

I DON'T BELIEVE IT.

I JUST WATCHED YOU FIGHT.

I'M NO GOOD WITH SWORDS.

BUT I'M PEERLESS WITH THE BOW.

YA HEAR THAT? LITTLE GREENY'S TALKIN' BIG AGAIN.

PEERLESS WITH THE BOW, EH?

I THOUGHT I WARNED YOU NOT TO BOAST, CHAPRA.

 I LOST TO YOU IN THE SWORD FIGHT. BUT I WON'T LOSE WITH A BOW!

 AND IF THIS IS HOOEY? HANG ME UPSIDE DOWN IF YOU LIKE.

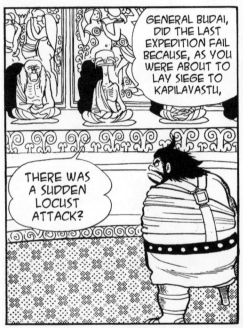 GENERAL BUDAI, DID THE LAST EXPEDITION FAIL BECAUSE, AS YOU WERE ABOUT TO LAY SIEGE TO KAPILAVASTU,

THERE WAS A SUDDEN LOCUST ATTACK?

 I'M SORRY TO SAY THAT EVEN OUR ELITE TROOPS COULD NOT FIGHT LOCUSTS.

 HMM A LOCUST SWARM...

 I TAKE FULL RESPONSIBILITY. GIVE ME ONE MORE CHANCE... NO, IT'S NOT YOUR FAULT, BUT...

 ...THERE HAVE BEEN STRANGE THINGS HAPPENING AROUND KAPILAVASTU RECENTLY. WHAT?

THOUGH IT IS, AS YOU KNOW, DROUGHT SEASON, WATER SUDDENLY SPOUTED FROM A MOUNTAIN NEAR KAPILAVASTU AND POURED INTO THE VALLEY BELOW.

A LOCAL REPORTED A TIGER WHITE AS COTTON LOPING IN THE JUNGLE!

A WHITE TIGER BEARS DIVINE TIDINGS.

SOMETHING MOMENTOUS IS ABOUT TO HAPPEN AT KAPILAVASTU – PERHAPS AN AUSPICIOUS EVENT FOR WHICH THE GODS ARE PROTECTING THE CASTLE.

179

FOR NOW, THE KING HAS DECREED THAT ALL ATTACKS ON KAPILAVASTU BE HALTED.

WHAT IN THE—

OUR MIGHTY KOSALA...

BOWING TO PUNY KAPILAVASTU? WE WILL BE THE LAUGHING-STOCK OF THE WORLD!

KING'S ORDERS.

I SEE, I AM OF NO USE IN TIMES OF PEACE.

IF THE WAR IS OVER, YOU HAVE NO NEED FOR ME.

FATHER, ARE YOU OK?

HM... CHAPRA'S COME TO GREET ME?

HOW'S THE TRAINING GOING?

I'M NO GOOD YET...

THE CAPTAIN'S TOUGH...

BUT I LIKE HIM.

HE THINKS ONLY OF TURNING OUT THE WORLD'S BEST SOLDIERS.

BUT THE WORLD'S CHANGING...

PEACE, HUH?

WE SOLDIERS...

ARE OF NO USE IN PEACE.

I WANTED YOU TO FOLLOW IN MY FOOTSTEPS AS A STOUT WARRIOR,

BUT THAT NO LONGER SEEMS WISE OR NECESSARY. KOSALA WOULD BE BETTER SERVED IF YOU BECAME AN ABLE SCRIBE.

FATHER, I HATE CIVIL SERVANTS. MY DREAM IS TO SUCCEED YOU AS GENERAL.

OUT OF THE WAY!

MOVE!

WANT TO BE CRUSHED?

ARGH! OUTTA MY WAY!

THIS IS HOW.

HUH...

THANK YOU.

CHAPRA, WHY DID YOU HELP THAT SLAVE?

THAT DIRTY SLAVE!

A TRUE WARRIOR, NO, ANY COMMON MAN WOULD IGNORE A SLAVE

OR KICK HIM OUT OF THE WAY...

NO, IT CAN'T BE...

... ...

CHAPRA, ARE YOU A...

WERE YOU...

A SHUDRA (SLAVE)?!

YES... SIR...

I DIDN'T WANT TO KNOW.

A SHUDRA, LOWEST OF THE CASTES!

MY SON, NOT EVEN A CITIZEN!!

WHAT HAVE I...

YOU HAVEN'T TOLD ANYONE ELSE?

NO.

I WILL FORGET THIS.

DO YOU KNOW WHAT WILL HAPPEN IF ANYBODY FINDS OUT?

KEEP YOUR MOUTH SHUT TIGHT AS A CLAM. THIS MUST REMAIN A SECRET.

EVEN IF YOUR BIRTH PARENT SHOULD APPEAR, IT'S FOR YOUR OWN GOOD.

THANK YOU, FATHER.

SO CHAPRA, LET'S SEE SOME OF THAT FAMOUS ARCHERY.

IF YOU SCREW UP, YOU DANGLE FROM THIS TREE.

FINE..

TAKE THIS BOW.

OOPS

187

TH-THIS BOW - I'M NOT USED TO IT!

I'D HIT THEM ALL IF I THREW THE ARROWS BY HAND!

REALLY! BELIEVE ME!

REMEMBER OUR PROMISE?

HELP! NOT THAT! GIVE ME A BREAK!

GENERAL BUDAI'S SON DANGLING FROM A TREE - HA HA HA!

THIS'LL TEACH YOU TO STOP BRAGGING, YOUNG MASTER.

IT WAS THAT CHEAP BOW! STONES WOULD SERVE ME BETTER.

HUH?

189

SAY THAT AGAIN!

WHAT CHEAP BOW?

THIS IS MY BOW!

BRING HIM DOWN.

YOU SAY STONES WOULD BE BETTER?!

GRAB SOME THEN, CHAPRA.

TRY AND BEAT MY BOW.

...
...

HEY, GIVE THE LAD A BREAK.

HE'S JUST A FOOL.

NO, HE INSULTED MY BOW. I WON'T STAND FOR IT.

I'M GOING TO PIERCE HIS HAND. HE'S GOT TO LEARN THE LESSON.

CHAPRA, DON'T! APOLOGIZE!!

CLANG!

KLUM!

CHAPRA!! YOU AREN'T USING YOUR SHIELD ENOUGH!

HAVE YOU FORGOTTEN YOUR LESSONS?!

WHAT ARE YOU HIDING UNDER THAT SHIELD?

SHOW ME!

WHAT'S WRONG WITH YOUR SKIN?

CAPTAIN, HE'S BEEN PRACTICING ARCHERY SEVEN HOURS A NIGHT.

194

MOMS, STOP! IF WE GO ANY FURTHER WE'LL KEEL OVER AND DIE.

NO, I'M HANGING ON UNTIL I SEE MY CHAPRA AGAIN.

TATTA'S RIGHT.

THERE'S NOT A DROP TO DRINK NOR A MORSEL TO EAT ALONG THIS WAY. WE CAN'T GO ON.

DIDN'T CHAPRA TAKE THIS ROAD TO KOSALA?

IF MY BOY MADE IT, THEN WHY CAN'T I TOO?

BUT HE WENT ON HORSEBACK OR ON AN ELEPHANT WITH THE ARMY... NOT ON FOOT.

EVEN IF MY BODY WITHERS ON THE WAY, I MUST SEE HIM AGAIN.

OH, MAN.

MOMS, DO YOU NOT LIKE ME?

YOU'RE NOT HAPPY BEING MY MOTHER?

I LIKE YOU, TATTA. BUT MY CHAPRA LOOKS JUST LIKE HIS DEAD FATHER.

DAWN WILL BREAK SOON.

AND WITH IT WILL COME ANOTHER DAY OF BLISTERING HEAT!

STILL
WE
GO?

YES.

IF WE DON'T
FIND FOOD AND
WATER TODAY,
ALL THREE
OF US ARE
DONE FOR.

IT'S A BIGGIE.

LOOK AT ALL THE EGGS IT'S CRADLING!

IT LOOKS REALLY WEAK. IT MUST BE NEARLY DEAD FROM HUNGER.

IT WON'T BE ABLE TO HARM US.

LET'S TAKE SOME OF THE EGGS, THEY'LL GIVE US STRENGTH.

HA, YOU'RE PRETTY GREEDY FOR A MONK. THOUGHT IT'D GIVE UP EGGS FOR FREE?

BUT IT HAS SO MANY! COULDN'T IT SPARE A FEW?

LET'S ASK FOR SOME THEN.

SURE... IF WE SPOKE THE TONGUE OF SNAKES...

I ENTERED THE SNAKE'S MIND AND ASKED.

IT'LL GIVE US SOME, BUT IN RETURN

IT WANTS ONE OF US.

IT'S DYING OF HUNGER AND WANTS TO SWALLOW ONE OF US HUMANS.

IF ONE OF US GETS EATEN, THE OTHER TWO WILL LIVE.

IT CAN'T JUST EAT ITS EGGS?

A SNAKE'S NOT GONNA EAT ITS OWN BABIES.

BUT IT DOESN'T MIND GIVING US SOME OF THE EGGS IN A TRADE. A HUMAN MEAL WILL GIVE IT STRENGTH TO LAY MORE EGGS.

LET'S DRAW STRAWS.

SHORTEST DRAW GETS EATEN BY THE SNAKE.

HA HA HA, MINE'S THE SHORTEST!

TATTA!! THAT WAS RIGGED!

WELL, I'M THE BEST CHOICE. MOTHER'S SEARCHING FOR CHAPRA, AND IT WOULDN'T BE COOL FOR A MONK TO GET EATEN BY A SNAKE!

BYE-BYE NOW... TAKE CARE, MOMS.

SAY HI TO BRO WHEN YOU SEE HIM.

COME AND GET ME.

I'M SMALL AND EASY TO SWALLOW.

TATTA!!

MOTHER FORBIDS THIS!

DON'T WORRY.

THE INSIDE OF ITS MOUTH IS SO COLD.

HE, HE, HE... I CAN'T SAY THIS FEELS PLEASANT.

I'M BEING SUCKED AT.

CHOMP

TATTA

YOU CAN'T DIE!!

NO NEED TO FEEL BAD – GOTTA HELP EACH OTHER OUT.

DON'T FORGET THE EGGS.

TAKE IT EASY.

GULP

TATTA!!

I CAN'T LET HIM DIE.

I'LL GO INSTEAD.

TATTA! LET ME TAKE YOUR PLACE!

I WAS A FOOL AND A COWARD. LITTLE TATTA! WHILE YOU CHOSE DEATH BRAVELY, I KNEW NOT WHAT TO DO!

HOW COULD YOU SACRIFICE YOURSELF SO CALMLY?!

MASTER ASITA! THIS CHILD HAS SHOWN ME THE WAY!

UNTIL NOW, I'VE CONSIDERED ONLY THE HUMAN WORLD. THAT IS WHY I COULD NOT UNDERSTAND WHY A RABBIT SACRIFICED ITSELF TO SAVE A HUMAN...

IN NATURE, HUMANS AND BEASTS, EVEN SNAKES, ARE ALL KIN.

HELPING EACH OTHER IS THE LAW OF THE LIVING.

NOW I SEE THAT, THROUGH THIS CHILD'S ACT.

CHAPTER SIX

THE KING'S CUP

WHEESH

TATTA!!

217

OH, TATTA...

YOU TWO ARE IDIOTS.

YO, MONK! USE YOUR HEAD.

WHY WERE YOU ALL FUSSING OVER SOME STUPID TRADE?

WHY NOT KILL THE SNAKE AND EAT IT?

SIZZLE

SIZZLE

SIZZLE

SIZZLE

EAT

HUH, DON'T WANT ANY?

WON'T GET ANY ALMS HANGING OUT IN THIS WASTELAND, MONK.

WHO ARE YOU?

WHAT BRINGS YOU HERE?

I'M ON MY WAY TO KOSALA.

GENERAL BUDAI OF KOSALA

HAS A SON NAMED CHAPRA.

WHAT DID YOU SAY?

CHAPRA? BUT HE IS...

CHAPRA'S MY CHILD!

OH YEAH, SLAVE WOMAN?

HA HA. CHAPRA A SLAVE'S SON?

GIMME A BREAK.

CHAPRA'S THE SON OF A GENERAL BY OFFICIAL DECREE. WHAT'S MORE, RUMOR HAS IT HE'S THE GREATEST ARCHER UNDER THE SUN.

CHAPRA IS NO ONE ELSE'S CHILD. HE'S MY...MY...

ZIP IT, WENCH!

I CAN'T STAND THAT RUMOR.

WORLD'S GREATEST ARCHER? AS IF!

I'LL SET THE RECORD STRAIGHT WITH HIM.

THE WORLD'S BEST ARCHER...

IS RIGHT HERE.

IF YOU MAKE IT TO KOSALA, DON'T MISS THE MATCH!

CHAPRA THE SON OF A GENERAL?

WH—WHAT CAN THAT MEAN? I HOPE IT'S SOME SORT OF MISTAKE...

CHAPRA, MY ARROW'S AIMED AT YOUR ARROGANT LITTLE HEART!

I'LL SHOW YOU WHO'S REALLY THE BEST!

221

KOSALA KINGDOM: SAVATTHI

IN THE FAR CORNER, GENERAL BUDAI'S SON, WEIGHING IN AT 110 POUNDS, MASTER CHAPRAAA!

FIRST ROUND: ARCHERY.

VINDIKA CHAPRA

VINDIKA FIRST. 3 ARROWS FOR 3 TARGETS!

Gallop Gallop Gallop

THREE HITS. NEXT IS CHAPRA. SAME NUMBER OF ARROWS AND TARGETS.

227

CLING CLING CLING CLING CLING

GNAW

PANT PANT PANT PANT PANT PANT

CLAP CLAP CLAP CLAP

VINDIKA

CHAPRA

I'VE TRIED TO WARN HIM MANY TIMES, BUT HE'S HEADSTRONG...

THAT CONCLUDES TODAY'S COMPETITION. AT DAYBREAK, WE CONTINUE WITH A TEST OF STRENGTH AND WRESTLING.

HOW DID I DO, FATHER?

JUST LIKE I DID WHEN I WAS YOUNG.

SIR, YOUR AUTO-GRAPH!

ME TOO...

LOOK HOW BUSY OUR STAR IS.

THE VIZIER PRAISED YOU. HE SAID THE KING'S CUP IS MOST LIKELY YOURS...

OF COURSE IT IS.

BUT, SON,

STRENGTH ALONE DOES NOT MAKE A HERO.

FATHER, IT'S JUST THAT I WANT TO LIVE UP TO YOUR GREAT WARRIOR NAME!

THAT'S FINE, BUT,

232

WATCHING YOU, I'M NOT SURE YOUR MOTIVES ARE GOOD.

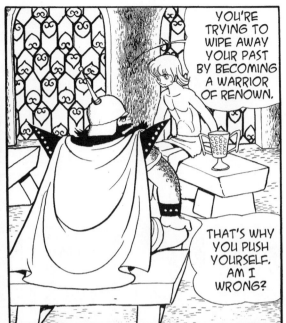

YOU'RE TRYING TO WIPE AWAY YOUR PAST BY BECOMING A WARRIOR OF RENOWN.

THAT'S WHY YOU PUSH YOURSELF. AM I WRONG?

IT'S AS IF YOU'RE TRYING TOO HARD

MY PAST HAS NOTHING TO DO WITH IT!

I AM WARRIOR CHAPRA, SON OF GENERAL BUDAI. THAT'S ALL THAT MATTERS!

...

HOW CAN I HELP YOU?

UM, THIS IS FOR MASTER CHAPRA...

?

GOOD LUCK... I-I'M A HUGE FAN OF YOURS.

HA! THAT WAS THE VIZIER'S DAUGHTER, PRINCESS MALIKKA.

SHE'S THE MOST BEAUTIFUL PERSON I'VE EVER MET!!

IS SHE REALLY HUMAN?

SHE WASN'T SOME FLOWER SPIRIT IN DISGUISE?

HA HA, MY DEAR SON, NO.

SHE IS THE VIZIER'S ONLY CHILD, HE'D GLADLY DIE FOR HER.

STOP WITH THAT FACE!

WHO IS IT? WHO ADORNS MY BALCONY WITH FLOWERS?

MASTER CHAPRA?

A RETURN GIFT ...

YOU GAVE ME BUTTERCUPS, WHICH ARE THE FLOWER OF CONGRATU-LATIONS.

I GIVE YOU OLEANDER. I HAVE HEARD THAT THEY ARE THE FLOWER OF DEVOTION.

NO, DON'T GO YET...

PRINCESS MALIKKA, I WILL WIN TOMORROW. PLEASE BE THERE!

239

240

VINDIKA HAS WON THE TEST OF STRENGTH.

NO!! I'VE GOT TO WIN!!

THE LAST ROUND IS WRESTLING. CONTESTANTS, ENTER THE RING.

COME ON, CHAPRA!

GO CHAPRA!

ROAR ROAR

GO VINDIKA!

NOW

HUP

HANG IN THERE, CHAPRA!!

THE KING'S CUP IS WITHIN REACH!

245

ROAR ROAR

CHAPRA!

YOU DID IT, MY SON! WHAT A COMEBACK!

VINDIKA: 2 POINTS. CHAPRA: 3 POINTS.

THE WINNER IS CHAPRA.

MASTER CHAPRA, SON OF BUDAI, WE BESTOW UPON YOU THE TITLE OF CHAMPION IN RECOGNITION OF YOUR SKILL AND VALOR, SECOND TO NONE IN ALL OF KOSALA. ACCEPT THIS CUP FROM THE KING.

RIGHT THIS WAY...

247

THE KING'S CUP...

NOW I AM ONE OF THE ELITE...

MOTHER! MOTHER, LOOK!

I'VE MOVED UP, LIKE I PROMISED! AND I'M NOT DONE YET...

ONE DAY, THAT THRONE TOO...

YES. ONE DAY I WILL BE KING!!

248

CHAPTER SEVEN

THE BIRTH

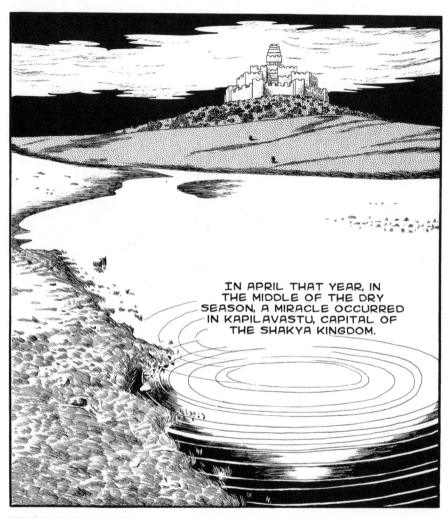

IN APRIL THAT YEAR, IN THE MIDDLE OF THE DRY SEASON, A MIRACLE OCCURRED IN KAPILAVASTU, CAPITAL OF THE SHAKYA KINGDOM.

THE ROHINI RIVER, WHICH MARKED ITS BORDER, DID NOT DRY UP DESPITE THE 110-DEGREE HEAT.

PEOPLE WHISPERED THAT IT HAD TO BE A GOOD OMEN.

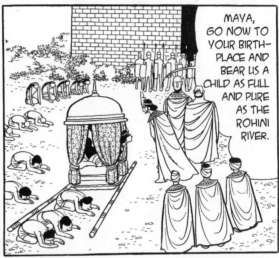

MAYA, GO NOW TO YOUR BIRTH-PLACE AND BEAR US A CHILD AS FULL AND PURE AS THE ROHINI RIVER.

KING SUDDHODANA'S WIFE MAYA WAS FROM THE RELATED KOLIYA TRIBE.

SHE SET OUT FOR HER HOMETOWN IN KOLIYA TO GIVE BIRTH.

251

TODAY IS THE 7TH OF APRIL...

KOLIYA IS JUST BEYOND THE RIVER. SHE SHOULD ARRIVE AT HER PARENTS' BY THE 12TH OR 13TH.

MEANWHILE, WHAT DOES ALL THIS STRANGENESS PORTEND?

NOT ONLY IS THE RIVER FLOWING, BUT FISH AND FOWL HAVE GATHERED.

AND ON THE SHORE, BEASTS...

...WHO SEEM TO BE SEEING MAYA OFF...

252

O HEAVEN – O EARTH! MAY YOU BLESS THIS CHILD TO COME – THIS WONDROUS CHILD OF MINE!

HURRY! WE'VE GOT TO REACH KOLIYA AS SOON AS POSSIBLE!

HURRY!

254

OH...
UH...
AHHH...

MY LADY!

SHE IS HAVING CONTRAC-TIONS!

WHAT? BUT WE'VE ONLY JUST CROSSED THE RIVER!

WE'RE NOT THERE YET?

WE ARE NOT TOO FAR, MY LADY.

OH! OOO, OH...

255

OOO, UHH...

HOW IS SHE DOING?

HER PANGS SHOW NO SIGN OF ABATING. SHE WILL BE GIVING BIRTH VERY SOON.

STRANGE, HUH? NOT THE SLIGHTEST BREEZE. NOT ONE LEAF RUSTLES.

AND LOOK ABOUT. 'TIS NIGHT AND YET LIGHT SEEMS TO FALL ON US.

BUT WHY IS IT SO BRIGHT? WHERE IS THE LIGHT COMING FROM?

LOOK AT THAT!!

LIGHT'S POURING FROM A CRACK IN THE CLOUDS!

BEFORE DAWN
ON APRIL 8TH,
A MIRACLE
FILLED HEAVEN
AND EARTH AND
ENVELOPED ALL
LIVING THINGS
WITH BLISS.

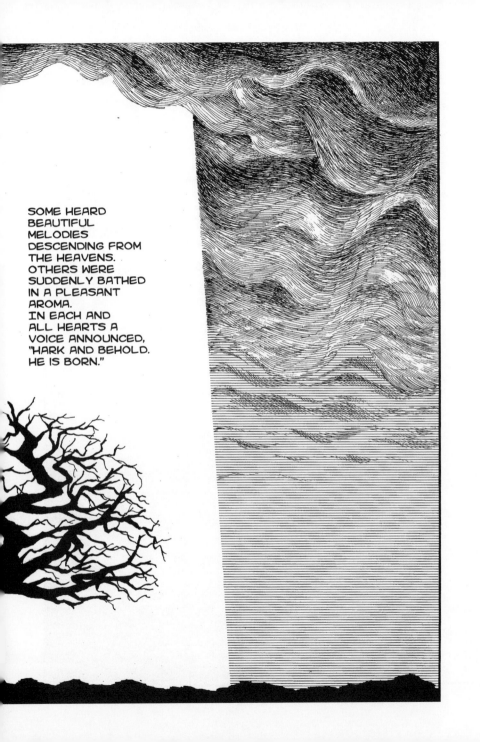

SOME HEARD
BEAUTIFUL
MELODIES
DESCENDING FROM
THE HEAVENS.
OTHERS WERE
SUDDENLY BATHED
IN A PLEASANT
AROMA.
IN EACH AND
ALL HEARTS A
VOICE ANNOUNCED,
"HARK AND BEHOLD.
HE IS BORN."

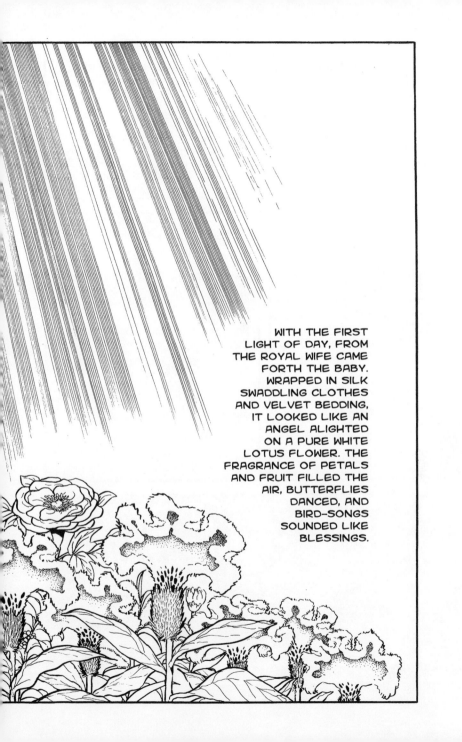

WITH THE FIRST
LIGHT OF DAY, FROM
THE ROYAL WIFE CAME
FORTH THE BABY.
WRAPPED IN SILK
SWADDLING CLOTHES
AND VELVET BEDDING,
IT LOOKED LIKE AN
ANGEL ALIGHTED
ON A PURE WHITE
LOTUS FLOWER. THE
FRAGRANCE OF PETALS
AND FRUIT FILLED THE
AIR, BUTTERFLIES
DANCED, AND
BIRD-SONGS
SOUNDED LIKE
BLESSINGS.

LADY IN WAITING, SHALL WE GO ON?

SINCE SHE HAS GIVEN BIRTH, THERE IS NO NEED TO.

LET US RETURN TO KAPILAVASTU AT ONCE.

WE CANNOT CARE FOR HER PROPERLY OUT HERE.

VERY WELL! LET US MAKE HASTE!

MESSENGER, SEND WORD TO HIS MAJESTY!

YES, SIR!

Giddeup
Giddeup
Giddeup

Giddeup

gallop gallop gallop

MY BABY BOY...

MAY YOU BE A GOOD CHILD...

GOO GOO

MY BABY... MOTHER FEARS THAT WE MAY HAVE TO SAY GOODBYE.

WITH YOUR BIRTH, MAYBE MY PART IS OVER.

I HEAR A VOICE CALLING FROM AFAR...

HEAVE HO HEAVE HO

RUN!

SEVEN HOURS LATER, THEY FINALLY ARRIVED BACK AT THE CASTLE.

YOUR MAJESTY! H-HER HIGHNESS!

MY WIFE?!

MAYA!

HONEY... HONEY, LOOK... HE'S HERE... YOUR BABY.

I THOUGHT OF A NAME ON THE WAY BACK

WHAT ABOUT SIDDHARTHA?

SIDDHARTHA... A GREAT NAME! "FULFILLING A PURPOSE," RIGHT?

HONEY... I CAN'T... I HAVE TO GO NOW.

GO? BUT WHERE? THIS IS YOUR HOME, MAYA.

HAS THE FEVER GONE TO HER HEAD?!

NO, MY HUSBAND. LATELY, SOMEONE'S BEEN CALLING TO ME OVER AND OVER.

WITH THE BABY SAFELY BORN AND IN YOUR HANDS...

IT'S TIME FOR ME TO GO, MY DEAR.

NON-SENSE!!

271

H-HONEY, OUR BABY BOY WILL BECOME A WONDERFUL MAN. IN ALL THE WORLD, NONE WILL HAVE A GREATER SOUL OR TRUER BELIEFS.

YES. I THINK SO, TOO.

THAT'S EXACTLY WHY YOU MUSTN'T DIE! IT'S OUR DUTY TO WATCH OVER HIM AS HE GROWS UP.

HONEY, HOLD MY HAND. THE MOMENT OF OUR PARTING HAS COME.

MAYA!

I WON'T HAVE THIS! STOP THINKING OF DEATH! MOTHER OF MY CHILD, MOTHER ETERNAL!

DON'T FORGET ME, PLEASE. I LOVE YOU, DEAR.

SHE HAS PASSED.

CARRY MY LOVE TO THE TEMPLE. ASSEMBLE THE PRIESTS. WE SHALL CONDUCT MAYA'S FUNERAL!

CHAPTER EIGHT

THE CONTEST

PLEASE TAKE THESE ALMS.

THIS CITY IS QUITE LIVELY.

INDEED. YOU'RE IN THE LARGEST CITY IN THIS REGION. SAVATTHI IS...

LIKE NEW YORK OR PARIS, IF YOU KNOW WHAT I MEAN.

THIS IS NIGAMA, A MARKET WHERE THEY SELL THE CASTLE'S LEFT-OVER GOODS.

A PARADE OF GENTRY.

YES. IT'S GENERAL BUDAI, A MAN OF GREAT INFLUENCE, AND HIS SON MASTER CHAPRA.

CHAPRA?

WHAT'S UP WITH THIS SLAVE?

REFERRING TO THE MASTER BY NAME?

WHAT WAS THAT ALL ABOUT?

SOME LUNATIC WAS RAISING A RUCKUS, SCREAMING "MY SON, MY SON"...

"MY SON"? ARE YOU SURE?

DESCRIBE THIS LUNATIC FOR ME.

YES, SIR: IT WAS A LOWLY WOMAN WITH A KID.

AND SHE REALLY SAID "MY SON"?

YES. IN HER DERANGEMENT SHE EVEN CALLED YOU "MY CHAPRA"!

WE HIT HER AND CHASED HER AWAY.

COULD IT BE?!

MASTER CHAPRA, A YOUNG WARRIOR SEEKS YOUR AUDIENCE.

HE SAYS HE IS THE BRAVE BANDAKA OF THE KOLIYA TRIBE.

281

...

IS IT THE CUSTOM IN THIS COUNTRY TO TURN AWAY GUESTS SEVERAL TIMES BEFORE GREETING THEM? ...ANSWER!

PLEASE FORGIVE ME, MY DEAR GUEST. I WAS OUT...

...
...

SO YOU'RE CHAPRA, HUH?

WHAT AN ARROGANT FELLA. HE'S GETTING ON MY NERVES ALREADY.

I'VE HEARD ABOUT YOU. THEY SAY YOU'RE THE GREATEST CHAMPION IN ALL OF KOSALA.

THEY TOLD YOU RIGHT. WHAT ABOUT IT?

THOUGHT I'D CHECK OUT JUST HOW GOOD YOU REALLY ARE.

WAIT A SEC! I DON'T THINK I LIKE YOUR TONE. WHAT DO YOU TAKE ME FOR?

SOMEONE TO HONE MY SKILLS AGAINST, THAT'S WHAT.

IF YOU CHICKEN OUT, I'LL SPREAD THE WORD. IF YOU FIGHT, YOU WILL SURELY LOSE.

ASSHOLE!!

HOW 'BOUT WE PICK A DATE AND A WEAPON? I'M WAITING...

OH YEAH? I'M CALLING YOUR BLUFF! AT NOON TOMORROW I'LL MAKE YOU A LAUGHING STOCK IN FRONT OF THE WHOLE CITY!

SQUAWK ALL YOU WANT TODAY. YOU KNOW YOU'LL BE THE BUTT OF EVERYONE'S JOKES TOMORROW.

DON'T WIMP OUT.

YOU!!

HA HA HA

HA HA HA

INSULT

WHAT AN INSULT!!

CHAPRA, WHAT ARE YOU SO WORKED UP ABOUT?

MALIKKA!

NOTHING, REALLY...

I JUST CAN'T STAND INSOLENT PEOPLE.

YOU'RE A HERO! OF COURSE SOME PEOPLE WILL ENVY YOU.

ANYWAYS, HE'S GONNA FEEL SORRY TOMORROW.

UM... THIS IS FROM FATHER.

WOW, PRECIOUS STONES!

PAPA SAID IT'S A GIFT TO MARK OUR ACQUAINTANCE ...

HE SAID IT'S AN HONOR TO KNOW YOU.

AS FOR ME, THERE'S NO GREATER HONOR THAN OUR BEING TOGETHER, MALIKKA.

THAT'S HOW I FEEL TOO... CHAPRA.

290

NOW FOR THE THIRD ROUND

ENOUGH! I'VE HAD ENOUGH OF THIS!

THIS IS CHILD'S PLAY THAT WILL GET US NOWHERE.

WHY DON'T WE JUST SHOOT AT EACH OTHER? WE'LL CLOSE IN ON HORSEBACK ALONG THE ROOFTOPS. WHOEVER PIERCES HIS OPPONENT FIRST WINS.

THAT'D BE A DUEL!

RIGHT. GOT COLD FEET? HEH HEH HEH.

I WON'T DUEL TO THE DEATH WITHOUT GOOD CAUSE!

I SEE IT NOW, YOU WANT TO KILL ME...

BUT WE NEED THE KING'S PERMISSION TO DUEL. HE WON'T GIVE IT.

OH WELL

297

WHISH

thwap

WE'LL USE THESE, SINCE YOU INSIST ON PLAYING AROUND.

ONE FOR EACH OF US, HAPPY?

GALLOP
GALLOP
GALLOP
GALLOP

WHOOM

READY?

CHAPRA!

NO!! NO!!!

OUT OF THE WAY! LET THE GENERAL PASS!

IS HE STILL ALIVE?

Y-YES, SIR, BUT BARELY.

SON... THIS WAS COMING...

QUICK! BACK TO OUR GROUNDS.

I MUST GO TO HIM!

NO WAY, MOMS, DON'T EVEN THINK OF IT! THEY'RE NOBLES! THERE'S NO KNOWING WHAT THEY'LL DO TO US IF WE EVEN ASKED ABOUT HIM!

I'M HIS MOTHER, TATTA.

WHEN A MOTHER MUST SEE HER CHILD, SHE DOESN'T CARE IF SHE'S A SLAVE!

EVEN IF IT MEANS DEATH, I WANT TO BE BY HIS SIDE.

I'LL SHOW THEM ALL WHAT BEING A MOTHER MEANS!!

I SEE THAT YOUR RESOLVE IS FIRM. I'LL COME WITH YOU. BUT PROMISE ME THAT WHATEVER HAPPENS, YOU WON'T REGRET IT!

304

CHAPTER NINE

ALL FOR A CURE

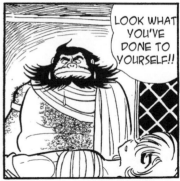

LOOK WHAT YOU'VE DONE TO YOURSELF!!

THE VIZIER IS HERE, SIR.

HOW IS YOUR SON? MY DAUGHTER HAS BEEN PALE WITH WORRY. SHE CAN'T SIT STILL.

PALE? YOU MEAN WHITE. CAN'T AFFORD COLOR PRINTING.

I HEAR HE'S BADLY HURT...

HE'S LOST A LOT OF BLOOD. THERE'S NOT MUCH WE CAN DO.

HMM...

OOPS, THAT'S ME!

IF HE HANGS ON 'TIL TOMORROW NIGHT, HE MAY RECOVER.

BUT... THAT'S NOT IN MY POWER...

CAMEO ROLE

......
......

WAIL

PLEASE ... PLEASE SAVE CHAPRA!! I BEG YOU!

WHAT'S THE RACKET?! QUIET DOWN!

SIR, I REPORT: A COUPLE OF TRESPASSERS SNUCK INTO THE GARDEN.

AN ALMS BEGGAR AND A SLAVE WOMAN?

FESS UP YOUR REASON FOR TRESPASSING!

PLEASE LET ME SEE CHAPRA!

LET YOU SEE CHAPRA?

HUH?

SHE... LOOKS LIKE HIM...

YOU MAY WITHDRAW. I WILL HANDLE THIS.

WHO ARE YOU?... WHAT IS CHAPRA TO YOU?

I ...

LET ME GUESS.

IS HE YOUR SON?

N-NO HE ISN'T, N-NOT AT ALL.

WE WERE JUST SO WORRIED ABOUT HIS CONDITION.

DON'T HIDE IT. YOU, WOMAN, ARE HIS SPITTING IMAGE.

YOU'RE HIS MOTHER, AREN'T YOU?

I KNOW CHAPRA IS SHUDRA BY BIRTH!

I WAS SHOCKED TO FIND OUT. IMAGINE THE HUMILIATION I'D FACE! THE GREAT GENERAL BUDAI ADOPTING A SLAVE AS HIS SON!

THAT'S WHY I'VE ERASED HIS PAST ALTOGETHER. THE SLAVE CHAPRA NO LONGER EXISTS! MY SON CHAPRA IS A GENUINE, PURE-BRED WARRIOR!

BUT HE IS MY SON!!

DON'T... BRING THAT UP NOW, FOOL.

I'VE COME ALL THE WAY TO THIS COUNTRY JUST TO SEE HIM.

PLEASE, AT LEAST LET ME SEE HIM... ONCE! LATER YOU CAN PUNISH ME.

I CAN'T LET YOU SEE HIM!

BE GONE BEFORE ANYONE ELSE SEES YOU.

I'LL FORGIVE YOU THIS TIME. GO AWAY!

AND DON'T EVER CALL HIM YOUR SON AGAIN.

LISTEN UP. AS MY SON, CHAPRA'S BECOME THE LAND'S GREATEST WARRIOR.

YOU KNOW WHAT'LL HAPPEN TO HIM IF IT GETS OUT HE'S A SLAVE!

...HOW IS... CHAPRA DOING?

HE HAS ONE DAY LEFT TO LIVE.

JUST ONE DAY?

THE DOCTOR'S GIVEN UP...

DAMMIT, I FEEL LIKE CRYING TOO!

GENERAL! THERE IS ONE WAY, ONLY ONE, TO SAVE HIM.

HMM... I RECOGNIZE YOU NOW. YOU'RE THE BRAHMIN NARADATTA.

MY MASTER, THE SAINT ASITA, SURELY KNOWS SOME SECRET WAY OF HEALING A MAN!

I CAN BRING HIM HERE...

OR HE COULD GIVE ME SOME SPECIAL DRUG.

SO WHERE IS THIS SAINT ASITA?

AT THE FOOT OF THE HIMALAYAS.

WHAT? ARE YOU CRAZY?

HAVE YOU ANY IDEA HOW FAR THAT IS FROM OUR KOSALA?!

EVEN ON THE FITTEST HORSE, A WEEK. ON FOOT, TWO MONTHS.

NO USE.

I PROMISE I'LL BE BACK IN A DAY. PLEASE, TRUST ME AND LET ME GO.

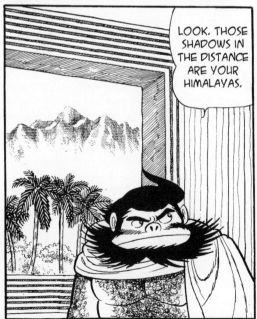

LOOK. THOSE SHADOWS IN THE DISTANCE ARE YOUR HIMALAYAS.

WE'LL MAKE A DEAL. IF CHAPRA DIES BEFORE YOU RETURN...

THE SLAVE WOMAN DIES TOO. KEEP THAT IN MIND!

AND IF I MAKE IT BACK IN TIME, AND CHAPRA IS SAVED...

WILL YOU GRANT HIS MOTHER HER REQUEST AND LET HER SEE HIM?

ALL RIGHT, I PROMISE. I'LL LET HER SEE HIM AND GRANT YOU A REWARD OF YOUR CHOOSING.

LOCK THIS WOMAN UP. THE MONK CAN GO.

NARADATTA

IT'S A GAMBLE. BUT DON'T WORRY.

TATTA TATTA!

HOW'D IT GO?

THE TIME HAS COME FOR YOU TO SAVE A MAN!

TATTA, YOUR SPECIAL POWER...

...HAS NEVER BEEN AS IMPORTANT AS IT IS NOW. GO TO MY MASTER ASITA.

WAIT WHILE I WRITE HIM A LETTER.

TAKE THIS...

SAINT ASITA LIVES AT THE FOOT OF THE HIMALAYAS. ARE YOU WITH ME? YOU MUST POSSESS A BEAST... A HORSE...OR A BIRD...AND GET THERE RIGHT AWAY. THEN YOU MUST SEEK OUT MASTER ASITA...

AND GIVE HIM THIS LETTER. HE'LL KNOW WHAT TO DO.

AND COME BACK BY TOMORROW NIGHT!

YOU GOTTA BE KIDDING!

YOU WANT CHAPRA TO DIE? THEY'LL KILL MOMS TOO!

OK... I'LL TRY.

316

317

TATTA!! BY TOMORROW, OR ELSE IT'LL ALL BE IN VAIN!

GOOD LUCK!

... ...
... ...

THAT'S A STRANGE HORSE...

Gallop Gallop Gallop

HEH HEH HEH...

WITH THIS LETTER IN MY HANDS, THAT CHAPRA'S A GONER! HA HA...

WHAT...

HEY, STOP THAT!

DAMN YOU!

GODS, O GODS!

TAKE MY LIFE, BUT PLEASE SPARE MY SON.

SIR, TELL ME HOW MASTER CHAPRA IS DOING? PLEASE!

ZIP IT!

IT'S NOT YOUR PLACE TO ASK!

TELL IT TO ME STRAIGHT. HOW IS HE DOING, AND WHAT CAN WE DO?

HIS HEART WEAKENS EVERY MINUTE. IF HE CAN BE SAVED, HE PROBABLY WON'T DIE. IF HE LOSES HIS LIFE, HE MAY NOT LIVE.

CUT YOUR MUMBO JUMBO, I TOLD YOU!

Gallop

Gallop

Gallop

329

HEY, WAIT. IT TAKES SEVERAL DAYS TO GO WHERE MASTER ASITA IS NOW.

OUCH, WHAT A STUBBORN HORSE.

GALLOP GALLOP GALLOP GALLOP

DANG... IT'S GONE...

CHAPTER TEN

THE PROPHECY

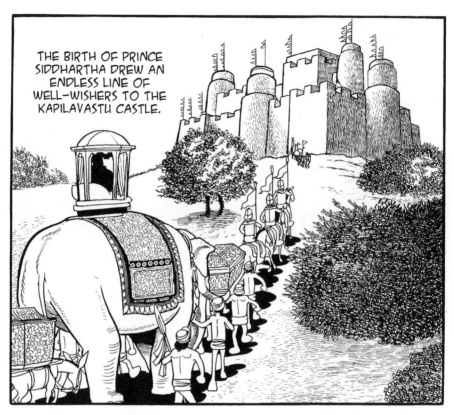

THE BIRTH OF PRINCE SIDDHARTHA DREW AN ENDLESS LINE OF WELL-WISHERS TO THE KAPILAVASTU CASTLE.

EARKNOB THE GREAT, KING OF NOWHERE, HAILS THE PRINCE!

KING FRAUD OF NOTALENT IS HERE WITH A GIFT!

LOOKS LIKE IT'S WINDING DOWN.

336

OLD MONK, WHAT GIFT DO YOU BRING? THE PARTY'S PRETTY MUCH OVER.

THERE'S NOTHING LEFT TO GIVE THE PRINCE.

NO MORE DIAPERS PLEASE!

I BEAR NOTHING.

BUT I HAVE COME TO DELIVER THE GREATEST OF ALL GIFTS.

WHAT WOULD THAT BE?

THE DIVINE BLESSING OF INDRA AND BRAHMAN.

HA, YOU ALMS-BEGGING GEEZER! YOU WON'T GET ANY LEFTOVERS FOR SPOUTING MONKISH CLAPTRAP.

BE GONE OR WE'LL DOUSE YOU WITH WATER!

337

WHAT?! SAINT ASITA?

SHOW HIM IN RIGHT AWAY, WITH THE UTMOST RESPECT!

MASTER ASITA... THANK YOU FOR COMING. THE BABY IS ASLEEP AT THE MOMENT...

AN INFANT DESTINED FOR GREATNESS DOES NOT SLEEP LONG. HE LIKELY STIRS AS WE SPEAK.

LET ME SEE HIM.

WHAT MEAN YOUR TEARS? IS THERE A BAD OMEN?

NO... I SHED THESE TEARS FOR MYSELF...

THAT FILLS ME WITH SORROW.

I WILL NOT LIVE LONG ENOUGH TO SEE THIS CHILD ATTAIN MATURITY, AND GREATNESS.

MASTER ASITA, I KNEW THIS CHILD WAS SPECIAL, BUT... YOU THINK HE WILL BE THAT GREAT A MAN?

INDEED... THIS CHILD MAY ONE DAY RULE THE WORLD. ONLY ONCE IN A HUNDRED CENTURIES IS SUCH A BLESSED ONE BORN.

MASTER, THERE CAN BE NO GREATER SAINT THAN YOU.

AH, KING... I AM NO MATCH FOR YOUR SON.

THIS CHILD WILL DO WHAT EVEN I COULD NOT. HE WILL TEACH THE WAY OF LIFE.

HIS WISDOM WILL ECHO THROUGH THE AGES IN PEOPLE'S HEARTS.

BEHOLD HIS FOREFINGERS: ONE POINTED UPWARD, THE OTHER DOWN.

HE IS CON-VEYING TO US THAT...

NONE EXISTS GREATER THAN HE, ON EARTH OR IN HEAVEN!

YOUR WORDS SCARE ME...

MASTER, I AM NOT FIT TO RAISE SUCH A CHILD.

DO NOT WORRY... RAISE HIM AS YOU WOULD ANY PRINCE. YOU NEVER NEED REPEAT WHAT I HAVE SPOKEN TO YOU.

WHEN HE IS READY, HE HIMSELF WILL SET OUT ON HIS TRUE PATH.

FAREWELL NOW, KING.

PLEASE, MASTER, WAIT. I BEG YOU TO STAY FOR THE FEAST!

I CAME TO SEE THE INFANT. THAT IS ALL.

HM?!

WHOOSH

344

345

THIS BIRD IS...

I SEE NOW.

TATTA... OR RATHER THE SPIRIT OF A HUMAN BY THAT NAME... YOU HAVE COME ALL THIS WAY IN THE BODIES OF BEASTS...

NARADATTA, A DISCIPLE OF MINE, MADE YOU DO SUCH A THING?!

NARADATTA, YOU FOOL... WHAT HAVE YOU DONE?

346

THE SAINT ASITA'S SOUL SHOT
ACROSS THE HEAVENS LIKE A
BOLT OF ELECTRICITY,
TRAVELING HUNDREDS OF MILES.
SIMILAR TO WHAT WE CALL
TELEPATHY, THE ARCANE
ART SENT A MESSAGE
TO SOMEONE FAR AWAY.

ZINNING

SLUMP

WHO CALLS TO ME IN MY OWN HEAD?

A DEMON OR A VOICE FROM HEAVEN?

NARADATTA

IT IS I, ASITA.

YOU SENT ME A MESSENGER, TATTA BY NAME, HAVE YOU NOT?

WHAT FOLLY! LISTEN WELL, YOU DUNCE!

TO SAVE JUST ONE HUMAN, YOU MINDLESSLY HARNESSED NUMEROUS BEASTS TO AN IMPOSSIBLE TASK...

AND KILLED THEM ONE BY ONE! THE BEASTS YOU BENT TO YOUR PURPOSE ALL SUFFERED GREATLY AND DIED CRUELLY!

YOU BELIEVE THAT HUMAN LIVES ARE SACROSANCT WHILE ANIMAL LIVES ARE WORTHLESS?!

351

IN LIKE LIGHTNING AND OUT LIKE A FLASH...

PERMIT ME ANOTHER APPEARANCE.

THE PATIENT HAS REGAINED CONSCIOUSNESS.

O GODS!

GARRR... GRRRR... ARR... ...

354

BAA~ BAA~

BANDIT?! A CRAZY BANDIT!!

NO, HE'S A WOLF MAN!

RRRAGH...

RUN!

UHH...
UHH...
AURGH...
6UH...
UH...

GOBBLE MNCH CRUNCH MNCH CRUNCH GOBBLE

GULP GULP

CHAPTER ELEVEN

THE JUDGMENT

HIS PULSE AND BREATHING HAVE STABILIZED. HE'S OUT OF DANGER.

THANK GOODNESS...

MY SON, CAN YOU SEE ME?

...

...

GOOD, GOOD!

WHERE'S THE MONK? NARADATTA?

HE'S GONE MISSING.

HE GAVE US THE RECIPE AND THEN JUST LEFT ALL OF A SUDDEN.

STRANGE FELLOW. AFTER DOING SUCH A GOOD DEED...

FIND HIM, BRING HIM BACK.

WHAT SHALL WE DO WITH THE SLAVE WOMAN?

SLAVE WOMAN? OH, HER, IN THE DUNGEON...

KILL HER.

WHERE'S THE CELL OF THAT SLAVE WOMAN?

HERE SHE IS.

SIR...UM... TELL ME, PLEASE, HOW IS MASTER CHAPRA? COULD THEY SAVE HIM?

LET 'ER OUT.

WHISH

CHA...
PRA...
SAID TO...

HE
TOLD
YOU
TO KILL
ME?

AND NOW
I'LL DO
EXACTLY
THAT, YOU
WRETCH.

AAAAH!!

STOP

THWACK

CHAPRA!

MOTHER!

M-MASTER CHAPRA!

WHAT?! DID YOU JUST SAY "MOTHER" ?!

AND NOW THAT YOU KNOW,

I'M SORRY BUT I'LL HAVE TO KILL YOU, MEN!

NO THANKS, MASTER, EVEN COMING FROM YOU, I'M GONNA HAVE TO PASS ON THAT.

GO AND REST, YOU'VE A BAD FEVER.

LET GO OF MOTHER. THAT'S AN ORDER!

MOTHER! WHY DO YOU CALL THIS SLAVE THAT?

FINE, YOU'RE AS GOOD AS DEAD, TAKE A LOOK AT THIS!

THE BRAND OF A SHUDRA!

Y-Y-YOUR MERCY, MASTER CH-CHAPRA. I WO-WO-WON'T SAY A WO-WORD.

X

BEHIND

CLING

CLANG

OW... OH... MOTHER...

CHAPRA!

YOU PULLED THROUGH, CHAPRA, O MY DEAR BOY, MY POOR LITTLE BOY! I WAS SO WORRIED!

IT WAS SO HARD... SEEING YOU AND NOT BEING ABLE TO CALL OUT TO YOU! I JUST COULDN'T TAKE IT ANYMORE.

AND HERE I THOUGHT YOU WERE SO HAPPY BEING A WARRIOR THAT YOU'D ORDERED MY DEATH... SO YOU DON'T WANT ME DEAD?

PLEASE, MOTHER!! DON'T EVEN SAY SUCH THINGS! 'COURSE NOT!!

IT WAS MY OLD MAN... GENERAL BUDAI... WHO GAVE THE ORDER TO HAVE YOU...

I HEARD HIM AND I WAS SHOCKED OUT OF BED.

THANK HEAVEN I MADE IT IN TIME...

CHAPRA, LOOK AT ME...

MY, HOW YOU'VE GROWN... AND SO STRONG TOO... THE WAY YOU FIGHT!

HAS MY CHAPRA BECOME MORE THAN JUST A LITTLE BOY...?

NOW WHAT SHOULD WE DO WITH THESE DEAD MEN? THEY MUSTN'T BE SEEN, OR ELSE...

WE'LL HIDE THEM IN YOUR CELL. IF ANYONE FINDS OUT I KILLED THEM, I'M IN TROUBLE.

THAT ONE... DAMN!!

SHIT!

MISSED HIM...I'M OUT OF PRACTICE!

MOTHER, LET'S GET OUT OF HERE, NOW!

I'LL LEAD THE WAY.

HELP

IT'S THE YOUNG MASTER...

DOWN IN THE D-DUNGEON.

WE'RE GOING THROUGH THE BACK WAY.

OVER THE WALL AND WE'RE OUT OF HERE...

FATHER
... ...

YOU IDIOT!!

SHOW IN MASTER CHAPRA!

BRAVE CHAPRA, CHAMPION OF OUR KOSALA, DO YOU ADMIT THAT YOU ARE NOT KSHATRIYA (WARRIOR CLASS), BUT SHUDRA?

YES, I DO.

OH

AH

OH

WHAT MADE YOU WANT TO BECOME A NOBLE, WHEN IN FACT YOU BELONG TO THE SLAVE CASTE?

ARE YOU REALLY SO DIM, MY HONOR? WHAT'S WRONG WITH A SLAVE WANTING TO BECOME A NOBLE? NOTHING!

I DON'T BELIEVE I AM HEARING THIS!

ONE CANNOT CHANGE ONE'S BIRTH STATUS! A SLAVE'S CHILD IS A SLAVE!

KSHATRIYA PARENTS HAVE KSHATRIYA, AND VAISYA (COMMONERS) HAVE VAISYA,

DOWN THROUGH THE GENERATIONS!

SAYS WHO?!

WHO? THAT IS THE WAY IT HAS ALWAYS BEEN.

AND SO WHO DECIDED IT HAD TO BE THAT WAY?

PEOPLE? OR WAS IT THE GODS?

ENOUGH, YOU SHAMELESS CHARLATAN!

GENERAL BUDAI, STEP FORTH TO TESTIFY.

GENERAL, YOU ADOPTED CHAPRA AS YOUR SON UNAWARE THAT HE WAS A SLAVE, CORRECT?

YES, SADLY, IT IS AS YOU SAY.

AND WHEN DID YOU FIND OUT?

SHORTLY AFTER HE ENTERED THE ROYAL GUARD.

AH, SO YOU KNEW, THEN.

WHY DIDN'T YOU CAST HIM OUT RIGHT AWAY?

CHAPRA IS A FINE SON.

AS A SON, HE HAS ONLY MADE ME PROUD. HE BORE ME NO SHAME.

DO YOU MEAN TO SAY THAT, KNOWING HIS STATUS FULL WELL, YOU ALLOWED A SHUDRA TO COURT LADY MALIKKA, THE VIZIER'S DAUGHTER?

GENERAL, DID YOU IN FACT, IN A SICK WAY, LIKE WHAT WAS GOING ON?

...

TELL ME, HOW IS CHAPRA?

AH... OH DEAR... POOR CHAPRA! DON'T LET THEM DESTROY YOU!

FATHER, I'M BEGGING YOU! PLEASE HELP CHAPRA, PLEASE, PLEASE, HELP HIM!

MARRY?

AS IN HE'LL BE MY SON-IN-LAW?

HELP!!

LISTEN UP. I'VE REALLY PAMPERED YOU, AND SO YOU DON'T HAVE THE FAINTEST IDEA HOW THE SLAVES LIVE OR WHAT IT'S LIKE TO BE POOR.

YOU SAY YOU WANT TO GET MARRIED, BUT DO YOU KNOW WHAT YOU'RE ASKING FOR? YOU'LL HAVE TO LOWER YOURSELF TO SHUDRA FIRST!

YOU'LL HAVE TO LIVE IN A SLAVE HUT AND DO LAUNDRY AND RUN ERRANDS FOR YOUR OWNER EVERY DAY.

THAT CHANGE YOUR MIND?

SOUNDS LIKE FUN!

HEY POPS, THEY'RE STILL AT IT?

GOT BORED, EH? IT'LL BE OVER SOON.

IF HE'S LUCKY, HE'LL JUST GET EXILED. BUT HE OUGHT TO BE PUT TO DEATH. BAH, A MERE SLAVE!

...

BY THE GODS, OFFER NOTHING BUT THE TRUTH!

ARE YOU SURE YOU GAVE BIRTH TO CHAPRA?

...

WAS THAT TOO HARD FOR YOU?

RESPOND! ARE YOU, OR ARE YOU NOT, HIS MOTHER?

THAT'S A LIE!!

I—I FOUND HIM WHEN HE WAS VERY LITTLE. CHAPRA DOESN'T KNOW THIS...

BUT HIS SLAVE MOTHER ISN'T HIS REAL MOTHER.

WHAT IS THIS? ARE YOU TELLING ME, WOMAN, THAT HE MAY NOT BE OF SLAVE BLOOD?

THAT IS SO, I ONLY RAISED HIM.

YOU'RE LYING, MOTHER! I KNOW YOU ARE!

MOTHER, I REMEMBER THE MILK OF YOUR BREASTS!

ABOVE THEM ALWAYS WAS YOUR LOVING FACE, ALWAYS!

PLEASE DON'T TELL SUCH A LIE JUST TO SAVE ME.

INDRA HAS BEEN CALLED UPON. THE VERDICT WILL BE IN VERY SOON.

THE VERDICT!

WHAT KIND OF NONSENSE IS THAT?

MY MOTHER HAS NEVER, EVER DONE ANYTHING WRONG! WHAT D'YOU MEAN SHE HAS TO DIE?!

ARCHPRIEST! HAVE MERCY! YOU MUST REDUCE HER SENTENCE TO EXILE AT LEAST! LEAVE US TWO IN THE DESERT IF YOU LIKE!

MUST YOU DISGRACE YOURSELF FURTHER?

IT'S OK, CHAPRA. I CAN BEAR DEATH...

AS LONG AS YOU KEEP LIVING, DEAR.

LIVE? WHAT FOR?

THEY'LL HAVE ROBBED THEIR UNMASKED SLAVE OF HIS ONLY TREASURE!

I'LL DIE WITH HER INSTEAD!

CHAPTER TWELVE

THE WALL OF DEATH

SLAVE SCUM!!

GREATEST WARRIOR IN THE LAND...HA, THE GALL!

LOOKS LIKE VULTURE FOOD TO ME!

CHAPRA...

MY SON...

CHAPRA'S BEEN SENTENCED TO DEATH, TOO.

WE CAN SAVE HIM IF YOU WISH. YOUR FATHER IS THE VIZIER AFTER ALL.

BUT EVEN THEN, HE'LL HAVE TO LIVE AS A SLAVE... A BANISHED ONE AT THAT.

WOULD YOU STILL BE ABLE TO LOVE HIM?

THIS IS IT FOR YOUR BEAU. WHY DON'T YOU SEE HIM OFF?

387

THE PROCESSION WINDS THROUGH TOWN AND THEN HEADS FOR THE EXECUTION SITE.

HMM

I'VE GOT TIME THEN... I THINK I'VE GOT A PLAN TOO!

YOU'LL LOVE THIS, CHAPRA. HEH HEH HEH

AN OIL FIRE!
SOMEBODY
DOUSED THE
CLIFF WITH OIL!

QUICK,
CHAPRA, RUN!
MOMS, HURRY!

SLIDE DOWN THE CLIFF! HURRY, CHAPRA!

TATTA, HERE WE COME!

THWACK

AAAGH

LOOK...

HEH, HEH, WE'VE BEEN PIERCED THROUGH.

BUT IT'S BETTER LIKE THIS... SKEWERED TOGETHER... DON'T YOU THINK, MOTHER?

WE'LL NEVER BE PARTED AGAIN, CHAPRA... NEVER...

CHAPRA!

OH...NO...
OH...YOU
STUPID...STUPID
SLOWPOKES...
DAMN YOU...

394